Contents

for Eamonn

'The best of life is lived quietly, where nothing happens
but our calm journey through the day, where change is
imperceptible and the precious life is everything.'
John McGahern

Harp Music
for Clare Roche

Song of a harp
sends chimes through
a restless air

even the dust settles
its hyperactive fleck,
pauses

follows sweet sounds
notes of pleasure
heavenly skill.

Strains of sorrow
yet all serene
transports gloom

to a dance and tune
breathing in, breathing out
stillness with each sound.

After it vanishes
let the final chord sustain
the equanimous again.

Sunflowers

I

'Prophets of the white sun' –
Michael Chase painted you
Monet, Nolde, Klimt, Kirchner,

and Bridget Riley too.
But Van Gogh understood your nuances in
Two Cut Sunflowers.

Ai Weiwei made a legacy to you,
Sunflower Seeds. The seeds
revered at the Tate Modern.

Then comes work
nourishment and hope,
your oil as commonplace as bread.

Despots could command
and be obeyed by you.
Enemies could mow you down

and shear each field
without a trace, a petal nor a sheaf
then feast on you,

claim your grandeur as theirs
in vases for decoration.
Then scatter your seeds to the wind.

II

In the Dordogne you do it all,
lift your heads in tune
with the rising sun,

move slowly upwards till at noon
you face the sky in open salutation,
relax in the afternoon.

The sky turns crimson
as the song of evening begins,
you obey each command

the orchestra playing you out
folded leaf by folded leaf
to the sun's golden rays,

till below the horizon
you tighten your corollaceous
and bow your corona.

Total silence now
end of the days symphony.
You sleep close, shoulder to shoulder.

St. Bridget's Day

Flight of small plinkings from a dulcimer
Like feminine rhymes migrating to the north
        From *A Brigid's Girdle* by Seamus Heaney.

This St. Bridget's Day welcomed
more than any gone before.
Trepid are we in this rite of Spring

after a night of snow and ice.
Below ever changing clouds of
grey and gold and white.

This moving rhyme
of feminine fertility
keeps us hushed

as shoots push forth
through wetness and wind,
long in their coming.

Rushes twist in St. Bridget's crosses.
We walk to her well to heal
a frozen welcome.

Listening

Our embroidered curtain
hangs over a door in the kitchen.

It's the one we made together.
In no other place does it look so well.

I had kept it hidden upstairs
beside my wedding dress.

Our curtain greets me through
the glass when I return

as it once did when it hung crooked
on that frame you made.

This house looks respectable
and not like that fixture

of wattles and wood
we inhabited in the Tibetan town.

The tree growing up through it,
river passing by, birds waking us at dawn,

nearness to work where you made clothes
of cotton, wool, silk and brocade.

You teaching me to make *thangka* trims
costumes, and the robes of ancient Tibet.

I've repaired some of the threads
on our curtain and taken up the hem.

It was fluttering in the draft
sending chills through my soul

whispering your favourite mantra
Om mani pedme hung.

I still listen to monks playing
long horns, conch shells and jawlings,

comforted in knowing these were
the last sounds you heard.

Gate

No wood to make a gate
no hinges to make it swing
but a beauty in these barriers
inspired invention,

a bed head no longer needed
the Herculean old man dead
his sons gone
his widow tending alone.

No barbed wire
to interlace with posts
or tie with Hessian rope
sink into infirm soil.

Headboard in the hedge
to gap gangly cows
before they sink into slime
to the shins.

Short horns rubbing scrawny necks
on the coppery armature
penning off tiny fields
neighbour from neighbour.

Wild roses, meadowsweet
decorating a boundary
fences only for cows
to gaze through the window

watching her kneading bread
on the deal table for sharing later

adding the only luxury –
a few raisins.

Dough caressed with flour
hung in the black oven pot
on the crook over the fire
turf tongued around it.

She returns to the fields
to chase the livestock back,
secures the headboard
with torn rags from flour bags.

Potato Apple Bread

I slice the apples thin.
Mother guides my knife
'almost like a wafer.'

She mashes floury potatoes.
They sit all day
to cool in the breeze.

Dusts the board white,
a snow of floured hands
knead and pat,

second nature to her
as the rhythm of
the rolling pin.

She lays Bramley slices
on the flat bread
adds a dash of sugar.

Another layer of potato dough
is swung in a flash
from board to griddle.

Movements, timing exact.
Her deft hands turn the bread
sacred as communion.

With calm and reverence
the cooling tray is stacked,
offerings for the family.

Breakfast time, early morning,
father eats
in sacred silence.

Storm

Clouds burst rainfall
hits our secret gullies
in this height of tidal flow,

floods itself in a sweep
running down our bodies
raincoats a useless defence.

Thunder cracks through our silence
a desolate song of summer
blips of lightening flit with no mercy.

When we surrender to walls of rain
that darkens waterlogged skies
bind ourselves against the wind,

it passes, freshens the air between us.
Intimate scents of turf and grass
opens a window of sun.

Hughie in the Hedge

Hughie lived in a hedge
sometimes he stood in it
and sometimes he hunkered down
often he scratched one leg with his foot
then he'd scratch the other.

He wore a suit and a flat cap.
Once they were brown
then they were green, like the hedge,
from moss and dew and wet.

When it rained
Hughie put his collar up
and turned his cap back
so that the rain ran down the peak.

Sometimes I'd forget about Hughie
in the hedge as I cycled by.

Then he'd step out – just one step
and say – *That's a grand bike.*

I'd stop and stand and we'd stare
at my Raleigh together.

With hands of green
he'd touch the handlebars.

Then he'd pat our dog Rover
and say – *That's a grand dog.*

Sometimes he'd take dry batch bread

and scallions and wisps of corn
from his pocket and chew on them
with rotting teeth.

Then one day as I went by
his spot was empty.
Hughie had died right there.

The next spring
primroses and corn
grew where he had stood.

Sliabh an Iarainn

Morning mist,
trees in a row
painted by Cézanne or Derain.

Patchwork of fields in different shades
of mauve – a colour that some say
doesn't exist.

Cinnamon, saffron, nutmeg.
Cake of granite, rendered and folded
changing minute by minute in a reflective sun.

Cloud above to tease you
move, dance and turn again
and fog your grey blue hue.

Some people meditate by the sea,
but you are far from the ocean.
No waves to erode you.

To contemplate in front of you
and send a silent prayer to Heaven
reminds us of a stillness long forgotten.

Wrinkled summit like the faces
of wise and silent men and women
who give all through steady endurance.

Risen sun reflects off white rock
like an oyster pearl
turns to a morning star new risen.

Translucent white cloud passes over
and carries on, leaving us to catch
glimpses of you, hour by hour.

You are there in our mornings
at our Angelus, our nights
and in our daily plights.

We go to your ridge.
No endless chatter here
silence, save the bleat of sheep.

And if we could live as you
cloud by cloud, sunset by sunset
we might know what it is to be still.

Coat
i.m. Akong Rinpoche

'Will you make me a coat
that looks respectable and rich
yet able to keep out
the winter of Eastern Tibet.'

We began to make a coat
gold brocade on the outside
three linings on the inside.

Rabbit fur, moss green wool
and a silken peacock blue
for the final trim.

We stitched and tacked and tailored
and stayed up nights
till we were sure

it would keep out the chill
of the winds, the cold of the snows
and still look respectable.

Finally we fitted him
with the coat before he left.
To top it, a matching hat.

Months later
when the snows had melted
he returned without the coat.

And when I asked him, he said

'I never intended to wear it.
It was for the old man

high up on the plateau.'

Honeymoon in Coalisland

For Tina Rock

With long red hair
buttermilk skin, eyes of green,
I see you walking with your husband
by the Lough shore
to the Holy River
flocked with rags for healing
from sphagnum
amber lichen, heather
and honeysuckle around you.

Grandmother of five now,
a young lady look
in your vintage Chanel suit
nipped in at your small waist.

I think again of your aunt
winding wool 'round
your young arms
for darning, mending
and knitting a matinée coat
for your first born,
click-clack of needles
as comforting as the smell
of rice pudding
baking to a brown crust
in the Stanley range
while you ignore the helicopter
and its search lights.

As you lay in love
by the lapping shore

under the patchwork quilt
threaded through patient hours
in dim nights –

I struggled with my *Oileán an Guail*
coming and going and going again.
You talk of it with ease
as we sip tea, read poetry,
and try to reclaim
those old clay chimney pots
with odd curls of smoke
rolling skyward.

Walking
for Alastair MacLennan

They've been talking about
you walking all day
in circles with your
head painted white.
It's snowing. Your black Zen mac
is drenched.
Performance Art.

You were walking when they
went to work at the docks
walking when they came back for lunch.
Quitting time now
you're still treading the same circle
around York Street.

They huddle in groups
and place their bets,
'He's praying', 'He's meditating
or trying to sell us something.'
'Or else he's feckin' mad.'
Beckett's ghost follows you
makes another circle
lets you float off again.

You stay in step with us
slow, steady, silent
mourning this city of broken dreams.
A human form masked
in white scrim asking
'When disaster strikes
do we wash the blood

heal the victims or polish the floor.'

Wearing soot for darkness
flour for light
dead fish for decay
empty vessels for noise
black balloons for falsehood.
Your images of troubled Belfast.

You do not forget:
Good Friday Agreement
day in May.
You tie lists of the dead
to the Ormeau Bridge.
The first memorial.

Waterfall
for O. R. Melling

Water falls in flung force
of a full forward flow

beside the riverbank
your current

sprays mint green grass
with a fine sprinkle.

This shady place
scented with buttercups

daisies and fuchsias, fresh
with moss and marsh

sturdy in the storm now passed.
Your deep torrents

gush in gallons
over rock and loam,

time to listen
to water flow

watch plantain
and speedwell glow.

Mist from hills whisper
be still... be still... be still.

Leitrim to Lough Neagh

He was always
curious about the swell,
the fullness, the flow:
bridges, inlets, islands,
the Finn, the Owenay, the Moy
and Gweebara Bay.

How the falls from Cuilcagh
and Marble Arch
converge and flow
from Fermanagh to Cavan.

But when my father drove
from Leitrim to Lough Neagh
by back roads,
no matter how many
near cuts he took
he mused
at how the distance
was always the same.

Jerry
i.m. Jerry Dowling

When sewing machines settle
and silence falls through golden threads
he points a steam iron into seams.

Hems, linings turned and folded
with the ease of a man
making hay or bread or love,

brushes the finished dress
perfected as he takes out pins.
Flicks the final tacks.

He sits then on the table
cross-legged, licks thread,
passes it through the eye of a needle.

The stitches live on
the labours endure.

Fishermen

They keep focus
on their catch
sailing on a currant

against the wind the dark the cold.
Their sky is filled with fading stars
weary in these weathers

they've travelled through for years.
Other lives inhabit this water,
unearthly beings

driven into the wilderness,
water spirits and ghosts,
as fishermen rock on the waves.

Drone of the engine
carries them home at dawn.
Shadows float off

leave them alone
to land their shoals
and lighten their load.

Time in the West

In the neighbour's kitchen
a shrine to clocks
tick and chime
bread rises on the range
kneaded like a prayer.

Men push boats
into the water and row
in rhythm with waves
movement slow
as if time is still
perfect like a Chardin.

Climb the mountain
past the bracken and bog cotton
turn again and watch
these people
deft at their work.
Fishing nets dry
like old hay on the sand.

Secret Language
i.m. Colette McAliskey

You enter my dreams
with softness and smiles.
I wake and touch your picture

tell you again:
Despite extraordinary dangers
life was still possible with you there.

I listen for your gentle voice
to speak our secret language.
A whisper tells me

no matter what
to remember the made up
songs we shared.

You're in a gentle place
the 'consummation of gnosis'*
where suffering has ceased.

*mystical knowledge

Women's Night
for Colette Lilley

Chenille cloth
on oval table
glows red.

They sit
on the settle-bed
by the fire.

Scent of turf
bannocks
and geraniums.

The old woman
leads them
'round the jamb wall

past her sullen son
who jukes
into the newspaper.

Battery lamp in hand
she digs the garden
uncovers a bottle

lifts her pinny
puts it in the pocket
of her petticoat.

Tiny tumblers
are filled
with *Harvey's Bristol Cream*

in the parlour.
Now she sings
The Rose of Tralee.

At *Danny Boy*
she stands on an orange box
for aspiration.

The women listen
in spite
of the dying air.

The corked bottle
is hidden now
in the flour bag

as she guides
them along the lane
in the autumn rain.

Soul Retrieval

Jurmey felt its hand
press hard on his chest
and a cold breath
on his face.

It was the strange paralysis
in his limbs
that made him visit the wise man
who said 'death has lost its way.'
Then he set about to pray
in dim lit days
rang bells
through windy corridors
as young boys
lay wide-eyed in fright.
This night grew calm
before lightening cracked
thunder clapped
and hailstones fell.

Morning: sun rose in a stretch
along the waterlogged sky.
The wise man fingered
his beads and said,
'Now the dead
is parted from you.
He has arrived
back on his path
and will leave you
as he journeys onward.'

Sean Nós

In the evenings old women
fishermen and young girls came.

They sang
while the guests ate in silence.

The singer held hands
with men on either side

to keep the rhythm
and 'earth' herself.

Each song took us
to different place.

They invited me into ritual
as they sang laments.

It was my baptism
into their *sean nós*.

Bardo – After Death

I dream she is baking bread
in the bardo which
lightens to a calmness

like incense on the shrine.
My brother and I wait
salivating from the sweet smell.

She is wearing pink lipstick
and goes for a walk
till the bread cools.

Now my mouth waters
in the kitchen
as I bake bread in my bardo

offer some to those gone before,
before I eat
your white light soda farl.

Secrets

Women walk close
by a hedge in the dark night
whisper their secrets

a time when souls are free
from clinging clans,
truth told in hushed tones.

Hands held, arms embraced
empathy – deepest longings,
frustrations at pretence.

Bosom touches bosom
sharing only
what women can

stop in the still air, intimacy growing
with each new confession.
Expressions on moon-streaked faces

darken with the sheer greyness
of what cannot be told
in the morning light.

Now, absolution, resolution
warm comfort
under silver trees.

The Little People

She walks
through a snow of bog cotton
orange rushes and scutch grass
over The Moss at dawn.

She sees before her
ink-blue water, stretching to the horizon.
Swans paddle side by side
near bushes and rickety fences.

'Is it the sea?' a stranger asks.
'No.' my grandmother says
'It's Lough Neagh
home to ghosts, banshees and fairies.

'The Little People appear in crimson coats
early, on misty mornings,
in a line on top of the water, dancing,
playing harps and flutes and mandolins,
as if they have been here forever.

'But they only stay for a while
before the sun dazzles them
and they disappear.'

She turns then,
and drives the cows home
in the light.

Man of the Lough

Tinkle of bottles churns and kettles
securing the thatch, held down
by fishing nets and oars.

Dogs bark and run at me.
The man of the Lough
leans over the half door

watches how I negotiate
a way through
field and bog and barbed wire.

'Have you no school to go to?'
he bellows. I reply
'Don't we learn from the Lough?'

His shovelled hands lift the latch.
Inside I survey it all again
the potato-sacked windows,

oil drums storing food
hang heavy
from the rafters.

Two goats sit like ornaments
on opposite sides of the crook,
turf fire warms the clay at their feet

I retire to the dusty settle
as he puts a mug of their milk
into my hand.

'Drink it up
it'll put roses in your cheeks
and chase the ghostly look out of ye'

His bed is straw
a fiddle above its head
not played since his wife is dead.

We walk to the water's edge.
He lilts at the Lough.
Silver wings flap

a common tern takes flight
its orange legs dangle
over the fairy tree.

Rainbows
i.m. Sherabpalden Beru

Starlings and crows
huddle in twos,

swoop, dive, fill beaks
return to their perch,

in communion
fan their tails and sing a lament

look about
eye the turquoise sky

fly through
a double rainbow two by two.

When one alone returns,
you have gone.

You who painted rainbows
which shine

in spheres of light
to a realm beyond.

Brilliant Red

First it snows
then it freezes
ice filaments
covering cobwebs
on window frames
fixed fast this filigree
stolid and still
pure as Chantilly.

Sunlight does not disperse
the dappled light over
tentacles of
thickened frost
and covered ivy
only holly berries brave
this white world.
One brilliant red cluster
a cameo

in the mantle of winter.

Rainbow Biscuits

I arranged a tea ceremony
a Tibetan exorcism,
invited the Lama
and our friends.

I made rainbow biscuits
with cochineal, saffron and blueberries
stacked them in towers
with candied angelica.

We brought these offerings
to the garden
requesting the spirits to move on
and wished them well.

The ghosts of two women
had passed through the galley kitchen
and into the old dining room.
One morning I rose early

and saw them through the jamb window,
my breath heavy on the glass.
They took the teapot and cups
from the China cabinet.

It began to dawn on me,
that was why when the air was clear
and stars were bright
I could smell tea brewing at daybreak

Chalice

It is hard to drink
the bitter chalice
when it comes.
Better to let
it sink in
and bless your neighbour,
for if he hasn't drunk
from it he surely will.

When the poisoned
cup comes
families conjoin
not through words
embrace or gesture
but with a glance
the knowing nod.

Boiling of the kettle
for tea that's never drunk
but for the comfort
of ritual incantations
rattling mugs
fussing over milk jugs
half eaten sandwiches
and untouched biscuits.

The sitting, the pacing
the mobile phone
to rescue moments
when tears well up
and spill over:
A wake for lost land.

Neighbours present
for each other
wait and watch and stay
the scalded heart
pumping veins
soothed by the presence
of loyal friends
whose distance and closeness
ebb and flow.

And when they've talked
or sat in silence
nibbled a ragged nail
we'll try another night
of fitful sleep
threading and weaving
these surrendered fields
tightly into our dreams.

Autumn

Stormy turbulent days as autumn returns
leaves fly through the villainous winds
the year grows old with a promise of
snow in transient white grey clouds
from now on everything withers and dies.

Vigour in work and fruits of labour
bring reward in the routine days
rituals of the season
time and space and honour
as the farmer gathers his crop.

Farther away on a different plane
glory and shame can vanish in an instant
as the light turns to darkness
or a warm breeze to a squall;
comfort comes and goes.

The sun once set will return
and spread its brilliance
the moon once risen
will shine a clear light
nothing lasts forever
not even the outrageous fortune of our time.

The Clock

The bedsit had everything:
an open fire with a companion set,
a Chesterfield suite
and a four poster bed.
The sideboard had ornaments
but no clock.

In the corner shop
I bought bread for breakfast
a galvanized bucket
and a copper clock with bells on top.

Handsome Sean came in,
the singer from the band.
I pushed the bucket out of sight,
embarrassed now that I'd bought
such a clunky pail.

I had told him I lived in a new flat.
With my hand on the door
the shopkeeper said,
'Don't forget your bucket.'

I stood motionless
as the bucket was placed in my hand.
The clock alarmed in it
and danced in the metal
loud enough to wake the dead.

One day I got up
and with the blunt end of the hatchet
stopped the copper bells from ringing forever,

racked the fire, slacked it up
filled the bucket with coal
and went back to sleep.
It was a Sunday.

Ghost

Footfalls echo in the memory
Down the passage we did not take
           T. S. Eliot, from *Burnt Norton, Four Quartets #1*

He will not arrive
with the hour of dusk
when spirits linger
in the air.
His walking laboured then
pushing past banshees.

When the sky is clear
stars are bright
and the moon shows new light,
he arrives late
his breath like ice
cold as his soul.

Frankincense and myrrh
from my tea-light burner,
calm the senses
slow the breath
slow the mind
drive evil out.

His face thaws
his dark eyes fixed
on the flame as he speaks
'Benediction again?

No ancient soldier
went into battle

without a paste of myrrh,
healed the wounds, so they say.'

I draw the curtains
turn our chairs
toward the fire
to allow the aromas to mingle.

When One Flower Blooms

We broke bread and water
for blackbirds, bullfinches and robins
only to witness all frozen again

as these creatures retreat
nestle, huddle and bed-in
beside the door, too frozen to fear.

Windows with a thousand curlicues
ice crystallized in silent air
striations of white over the street.

After an eternity,
clouds thickened over the hill
showers of rain darkened the sky

eyes gladdened by a single bud
in a forgotten flower bed,
quivering life about to break forth.

Us repeating a Zen prayer
'When one flower blooms
it is spring everywhere.'

Companions

She straddles the group
in her frocks and socks and wellies

dunging out the byre
wheels it away in the barrow.

Thin as a stick under
her layers of mens' coats

leans against the warmth
of a goat squeezing the teats

filling the pail
she'll never drink

but her tatty long-eared
dogs are happy to sup

as ducks and hens
feed by the pond.

Inside cats sit
on a range that isn't lit,

no cooking done,
she walks across The Moss

to shop for tea and biscuits
and sometimes ice-cream.

No housework
nor lighting of lamps.

Livestock give
comfort and company.

Caps and hats kept in place
with scarves and mantillas

as she walks the ramparts
in wind and rain and snow

climbs gates and fences
with no complaint.

Fit and independent to the end
quietly she slips away.

The animals mourn her.

Unrepentant Ones

The confessional where
confessions were never told,
the graveyard – girls behind
gravestones, smoking,
confessing passions of
the night before.

Mass, devotions, benedictions,
social occasions to flaunt figures.
Women made like Sophia Loren
and Gina Lollobrigida,
big-boned, big-breasted
small-waisted, curved hips.

Pillbox hats, Chanel suits
stilettos, well turned ankles.
Purple coats, orange mini-dresses,
blonde page-boy hair,
green seductive eyes.

Glances exchanged,
a grasp, a touch, a feel.
Fire and brimstone from the priest
'Sins of the flesh' he roars
'Bring them on' we pray.

Second Mass. The priest refuses
to serve communion
cursing us all
'Great prayers but bad payers
Oh, Glorious Clonoe!
You are all damned to Hell'

Snuggle close on the stairway down
hold hands, brush cheeks
'See you tonight?'
'Oh yes, we sinners
must all go to hell
together.'

Lost

'Don't go down the back road
you'll get lost at the place
where the bridge crosses
the stream by the stone wall
where the elder and hawthorn grow.'
My neighbour warned me.

Several times a day
I walk the back road
pick spearmint, chamomile,
wild bergamot, burdock and thyme
near the tall pines while the wind
whistles through them.

Recently I found St. John's Wort –
hypericum, which blooms
at the feast of St John the Baptist
known as the god of summer
vegetation and life,

who went into the wilderness
dressed like a wild man
feeding on plants and
became known as
the green man of fertility.

Hypericum – plant of the Little People
from the underworld, who
sometimes take mortals
to their kingdom and
teach them secrets of the natural world,
seership, rituals and dreamtime.

'If you walk in the woods
get turned around, and lost;
the Little People
are trying to get your attention.
Make an offering of food
and they will be appeased.'

I said, and gave him chocolate
to leave on the stone wall
where the elder
and hawthorn grow
as he'd walk the back road.

He turned away from me
and closed the door.

Cornucopia

Fire lights the October sky
red embers fly
an autumnal firework display
as we return from devotions,
the gypsies are here again
camped by the roadside.

We taunt and tease
and frighten each other
with 'They'll take you away'
cry it over and over
trembling in terror
as we run along the hills
back to our home place.

We walk the same hills
now after Cornucopia came,
vistas turned to ruin
oversized houses with electric gates.
If the gypsies returned
would they find a sally wattle
to make a bender?

The shortness of life
makes us blind
so often led astray.
Time and truth vanish like ashes
consuming each other.
The fire blazes on.

Front Door

Come home, new look wire grill on the door
Think of the days I followed her inside
As she led, I tiptoed along the floor
Learn by ritual: in me she'd confide.
Our door at home has many tales to tell
Clear glass revealing the forthcoming trade
Indians with cases of clothes to sell
Tinsmiths looking for pots to be remade
Or those days when we all ran out through it
To play in the snow on the lawn with dad –
Run back fast to the room with fire lit.
Door closing on the days when we were glad.
Nothing comes in now, nothing departs
Memories only held tight within hearts.

The Waves of Tory

The Orange Hall
at Markethill stands still.
Corrugated iron preserved
with airplane-grey paint.
Terracotta trim
blazes bright in autumn light.

Derrylaughan Hall
where we went to *céilís*
in our youth.
Its blunt tin holes
are a deep rust.
Wind whistles through
from Lough Neagh.

Tilley lamp hung
back then on a pulley
fading in the middle
of *The Waves of Tory*.

As we squeeze tighter together
before the priest hauls it down,
pumps with all his might
to cast blight on our intimacies,
then resumes his sentinel march
between us.

Follows us home,
our vanishing bikes
up loanings, down lanes
through gates, into fields
land in marshy drains,

confound him.

Its gone now
and we can't go back there
to dance *The Waves of Tory.*

Seana Feistín

By dawn wild ponies herd
gossamer manes flowing,
wide eyes bearing an ethereal look.

Black rabbits land on the window sill.
Donkeys bray as they knock over rocks.
Atlantic waves slap against stones.

Vigorously now, the wind whips
seaweed, deadwood and leaves
into a whirling carnival of debris.

Then misty calm on glassy sea,
no wave will lap or taunt
this stillness and light.

Children fall out of bed.
Women in black shawls
make their way to Galway.

'The *cois céin coilligs* are coming' they say:
The day is lengthening by the stretch
of cockerel's footstep.

Lough Neagh Breeze

We walked past the rowan trees
with the Lough Neagh breeze
at our backs

the promise of home
still distant in the crimson sky,
dimming light arrived too soon.

Scutch grass caressed
our ankles as we ran barefoot
on dried-out bogs.

A far-off wail –
'The Banshee' – the boys shouted.
We quickened our steps.

The yellow loaning
was hard under our feet
the threat of death imminent.

No words spoken now
as each of us turned into our lanes.
We ran the longest one.

Who would it be?
My mother my father or me?
Dusk enveloped our town land.

Onto the final sprint and home.
'We saw her, the Banshee.'
Mother cut bread

and shook her head
buttered scones and fried pollans
'Eat your meal and shush' she said.

In bed we listened
for those lonely shrieks.
Wind whistled in the ash.

Tashi the Tailor

From the stretch of his index finger
to the broad extremity of thumb
from middle digit to middle digit

with arms outstretched
in a rolling motion
his body measures the fabric,

rips the cloth along a perfect weft
sews, folds and presses
hard between his hands.

After days, the *thonga* is complete,
a yellow and maroon
waistcoat for the Lama.

He gives a *mala* to me of human bone
from his dead grandfather's hands
in gratitude for this place to work.

'Too precious a gift' I say.
His sturdy body steps away, offended
as I offer the rosary back.

So I rub the bony beads
briskly between my palms
then put them around my neck

and say 'I'd like to have met him.'
'You did,' he says
puts a knapsack on his back

walks out through the snow
and disappears
over the horizon.

Overcrowded Nest

Once I travelled to Connemara.
looking for a place
to serve tea and booked into a B&B.

Every evening in Carraroe
I talked with locals.
Exhausted, yet happy I fell into bed at night.

As the family slept,
a tiny girl crept in beside me,
squeezed out of bed by her siblings.

She snuggled beside me,
then disappeared before breakfast.
Her mother served soda bread and blackberry jam.

She spoke little and only in Gaelic.
Infused with place, and nourished
I began again, found a house

and created a restaurant.
Evenings – the fishermen,
old women and young girls came.

Many times till dawn we sang,
before struggling off to bed,
and even there the little one crept into mine.

In the mornings I learned to serve
soda bread and blackberry jam,
and soon spoke little and only in Gaelic.

Installation

Two goats graze in our garden
off the Lisburn Road in Belfast.

Each morning we put them into a horsebox
drive through Shaftesbury Square

along Royal Avenue, release them at Carlisle Circus
lead them by York Street to the art college.

Punks with pink Mohicans cheer us.
Shoppers laugh out loud, forget about a bomb

shards of flying glass and the siren din
which deafens women's screams.

The doormen try to stop us. As we argue with them
the genteel creatures foul the floor

with neat brown balls of dung.
This time we have an official paper.

It says *Goats Are Part of the Installation*.
The wide-eyed animals like the lift.

Free for the day to amble in a studio
where grass sprouts from migrant sods.

The goats graze on bales of sweet hay
then create manure to urge the grain on.

Jamsey

He surveys the hawthorn
by the road,
hears a the car
straightens his lapels

steps out
digs in his pocket
finds a rosary
and freezes in prayer,

each smooth brown
bead of wood
passes through his fingers.
The Canon stops

remains seated
stares ahead
unable to look
at this pure soul

yet bids Jamsey kneel
right there in the bracken.
repentant though innocent.
'Bless me Father for I have sinned'

The priest clutches a gold crucifix
and drives away.
Jamsey stares after him,
then steps back into the hawthorn.

November

Seasons turn and turn again
clouds thicken over the hill
showers of rain darken the sky
geese fly southward
crying their desolate November song.
It is autumn.

Starlings swoop and dive
drawing a curtain of speckled cloud
across this short season.
Soon trees will glisten with frost
crystallising the air.
The land will fall silent.

Soar with the starlings
or hover with the hawk.
The wise and foolish pass
through the same changes,
gladdened or saddened
by these natural things.

Japanese Moments
for Fuki Yoshida

Taught nothing
of sacrilege
nor sacrificial penance

she slices scallions
folds cinnamon and *kuzu*
into *mitarashi dango*

toasts wafer *nori*
that glistens brown like her eyes
reflecting the ocean between us.

She rolls and folds
rice, *umeboshi* plums
arami and *wakami* in bamboo

greets guests
with okra cake
and bowls of *bancha* tea

plinks
of her *sanshin*
send chimes

through the still air
even the kettle
stops its wheeze.

I pause now
follow her
every movement.

The Doire
for Edel

Pump freezes in winter
fired straw brings a gush
water serves us.

We hold the bucket
on her snout
brown liquid flows into foam,

walk on watery
swampland
as geese sing a stoic song.

This symphony of life
plays out through a helter skelter
of hailstones.

Sunlight melts snow
in Annaghaboe.
Sunset blushes

into spring.
Winter lifts its final latch,
swallows begin to nest.

Godmother

You cycle up the lane
in a tweed coat
past heather and damp moss
to milk cows on your hunkers,

wheel galvanised buckets
of frothy liquid back home
on the handlebars,
with an entourage of dogs.

Place soda bread
on the deal table
for goats to eat at.
They watch through the door

as you throw grain outside
to draw chickens from the old tram
stationary now, no seats
instead broody holes of hay.

Flagstones in your living room
worn with curvaceous dips
from the rasp of cats' tongues licking
milk in the dents.

A kerfuffle of kittens
run out, round the jamb wall
as you feed the copney pig
on your knee with a bottle.

The kettle sings a welcome
full with water from the well

on nights when *ceilliers* call
to divine stories from you.

Morning, we wake
to the rattle of your buckets
the warmth of laughter
as you turn your foot on the pedal.

Hot Water Jar

i.m Sheena Devlin

My brother looks like your brother,
hair sleeked with Brylcreem.

We looked like each other
petite, brown haired, fringed,

shared beds like sisters
warmed each others hands

as we played footsy
with an old hot water jar.

Never at sea
but always a ken between us.

And when clouds descended
you created a luminous space

stole darkness from the black sky
and let the stars shine through.

If I stay in the home place
I fill an old hot water jar

play footsy with it
and look for stars.

Dust on Dust

Lean and happy yet
leather aegis on his back.
I recognise him
after forty years.

He brings Antrim coal
that glows bright
leaves ashes
of silky white.

By hollowed flames
we were all together
lighting fires in a time before
for crabbed teachers

to keep them warm
as they grudged us heat
to thaw frozen milk bottles,
our only nourishment.

Where we were taught
catechism and how to pray
and little education.
Instead, a fear-swathed dread

of blows and insults
more acrid than ashes
or smoke from black coal
turned to cinders cold.

In spite of this,
you had stamina in your soul

survival in your heart
labour in your blood

to heave heavy loads
and fold cribbings.
Rev the lorry –
all empty now.

Blood Imprinted on the Heart of the Lotus

I
When the moon shone rings of light
and planets hung above the mountain
Chinese soldiers ransacked tents.

The nomads were the last to flee
across the border to Ladakh
echo of gunfire over *mani* stones.

The old and weak died on their feet
a prayer wheel in their right hand
and a *mala* bead in the left.

II
Tenzin gathered the remnants of his family,
created shelter, but the winters
froze ice into his long black hair.

Wind bellowed over dead yaks
the ones he'd bought with stones of amber
kept safe in his locket.

III
The family dragged themselves
through blizzards over Chumthang mountain
to a mud hut in a refugee camp.

Snow melted slowly in the kettle.
They recited mantras through freezing nights
as bitter winds cut into their bones.

IV

We bought them a cow. They named her Lhamo
and sang praises to her. Lhamo had calves
gave milk, was fed with hay carried for days over rock.

Tenzin worked in the garden of the monastry,
welcomed the Dalai Lama each summer
and plaited his hair with beads of moonstone.

Ancient Culture

Oils thaw our frozen feet.
Herbs soothe
our hardened hands.
Fragrant smells
ease our senses
in nights of storm

and allows moonstone
to reflect the candle light.
Our small bowls
on the shrine
are filled with offerings.

About the Author

Angela McCabe was born in Coalisland, Co. Tyrone, studied anthropology and psychology, skied in Switzerland, worked as a cordon bleu chef in Spain, and travelled overland to Lapland, through Russia, Poland and North Africa. Whilst running a small restaurant and art business in Connemara she made occasional trips to Eastern Europe, USA and Canada.

She became a social worker with underprivileged children in various parts of U.K., and lived in a Tibetan Buddhist community in Scotland where she learned how to make Tibetan art.

After gaining a degree in Fine Art she worked as a painter and Performance Artist. Trained as an Art Therapist, Neuro Development and Sound Therapist, Angela has practiced in Dublin, Belfast and Tyrone and set up a practice in Ballinamore Co. Leitrim.

Angela continues to work as a therapist, studies Tibetan philosophy and art, and helps with a Mongolian/Tibetan charity, writes short stories, screenplays and has made an award-winning short movie. She has received literature bursaries from Leitrim Arts Office and The Arts Council of Northern Ireland.

Acknowledgments

Some of the poems in this book have previously appeared in *Tuesdays at Charlies, Fermanagh Writers' Anthology; The Spark – Border Counties History Review Magazine; The Poet's Place* – Poetry in Motion, Belfast; *Moment* – Community Arts Anthology, Belfast; *Red River Poetry Review* (USA); *Jampa Ling Newsletters,* Cavan. *The Leitrim Guardian; The Leitrim Observer; The Tyrone Times; The Mid Ulster Observer; The Coalisland Democrat; Tails of the Unexpected – Bright Eyes Anthology,* Fermanagh; *Still Anthology,* Belfast Community Initiative.

Several poems have been featured on Cavan Radio and Live Streams for Poetry Ireland. *Listening* was Regional winner – FSNI Competition and *Sliabh an Iarainn* was winner of *The Leitrim Guardian* Literary Award for Poetry.

This collection was short-listed for the Bradshaw Books *Cork Literary Review* Competition.

The author greatly acknowledges receipt of a bursary from Leitrim Arts Office and a Support for Individual Artists Program from the Arts Council of Northern Ireland.

Thanks to Padraic O'Reilly, P.J. Kennedy, Teresa Wood, Val Whelan, Ann Gillan, Sue Booth-Forbes, Monica Corish and Brian Quinn.

Special thanks to Dermot Healy for his help and encouragement, as well as his invaluable editorial skills.

THE BANNED MAN

Shaun McCarthy

ALSO BY SHAUN MCCARTHY

Places   *Hippopotamus Press*